SABER-TOOTHED
TIGER

For a free color catalog describing Gareth Stevens Publishing's list of high-quality
books and multimedia programs, call 1-800-542-2595 (USA) or 1-800-461-9120 (Canada).
Gareth Stevens Publishing's Fax: (414) 225-0377.
See our catalog, too, on the World Wide Web: http://gsinc.com

Library of Congress Cataloging-in-Publication Data

Antony, Laurence.
    Saber-toothed tiger / by Laurence Antony ; illustrated by Tony Gibbons.
        p. cm. — (The extinct species collection)
    Includes index.
    Summary: Describes the physical characteristics and habits of this
fierce prehistoric creature.
    ISBN 0-8368-1596-3 (lib. bdg.)
    1. Saber-toothed tigers—Juvenile literature. [1. Saber-toothed tigers.
2. Prehistoric animals.] I. Gibbons, Tony, ill. II. Title. III. Series.
QE882.C15A57   1996
569'.74—dc20   96-4998

First published in North America in 1996 by
Gareth Stevens Publishing
1555 North RiverCenter Drive, Suite 201
Milwaukee, Wisconsin 53212 USA

This U.S. edition © 1996 by Gareth Stevens, Inc. Created with original © 1995
by Quartz Editorial Services, 112 Station Road, Edgware HA8 7AQ U.K,
under the title *Sabre-Toothed Tiger*.

Additional artwork by Clare Heronneau

U.S. Editors: Barbara J. Behm, Mary Dykstra

Printed in Mexico

1 2 3 4 5 6 7 8 9 99 98 97 96

the EXTINCT SPECIES collection

SABER-TOOTHED
TIGER

Laurence Antony
Illustrated by Tony Gibbons

Gareth Stevens Publishing
MILWAUKEE

Contents

Meet the saber-toothed tiger

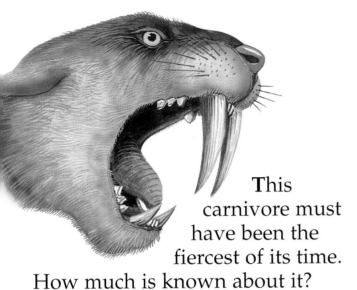

This carnivore must have been the fiercest of its time. How much is known about it?

When did it prowl the planet? What was its environment like? What did it feed on? Why did it have such large and sharp teeth? And why did it become extinct eleven thousand years ago?

Scientists have discovered a great deal about this predatory creature. Now you can share in this knowledge and become a junior saber-toothed expert.

The illustrations in this book are so realistic that it might seem like the **saber-toothed tiger** has come back to life. Watch out as you read on — just in case one leaps out from the page!

Fierce

The now-extinct **saber-toothed tigers** resembled the tigers of today. Like modern tigers, **saber-toothed tigers** were carnivores. They spent much of their time searching for meals of meat. From the study of remains, scientists can tell that these prehistoric tigers were probably even fiercer than today's tigers!

The best-known and most common member of the **saber-toothed cat** family was **Smilodon** (SMILE-OH-DON), shown in this illustration. It was about 4 feet (1.2 meters) long and had a fairly large head. The front part of its body was particularly muscular and strong.

Most noticeable of all were its huge canine teeth. These were like daggers with sharp, jagged edges.

They must have been a terrifying sight, especially since **Smilodon** could open its jaws widely to stab victims with awesome fangs.

6

carnivore

Early humans, armed with primitive weapons, were **Smilodon**'s main enemies. This picture shows how a child of today would have compared in size with a **saber-toothed tiger**.

Back in the

Most **saber-toothed cats**, like the **Smilodon** shown here, lived during Pleistocene (<u>PLY</u>-STOH-SEEN) times. This era began about two million years ago and ended about 10,000 B.C.

It was during this period that many mammals evolved into new forms, including humans.

This was the time of the last great Ice Age. Huge changes in temperature occurred, and the world cooled down. Enormous ice sheets moved from the North Pole to cover much of North America — as far south as where New York City is located today — as well as Europe and Asia.

Sometimes the ice would retreat from the landmasses. Vegetation, much like today's grasslands and forests, grew. But then more ice sheets arrived, and the landscape became a frozen wasteland again.

8

Ice Age

Africa and Australia escaped this Ice Age. Instead, these continents experienced prolonged dry and wet periods, one after another.

Many of the mammals that evolved in cold regions during Pleistocene times were large. They had thick hides or shaggy coats to provide insulation against the extreme cold. Under their skin, they had thick layers of fat as added protection.

Warm-blooded animals, such as mammals, have a better chance of survival in very cold weather. They can cope with freezing temperatures far better than cold-blooded creatures, such as reptiles and amphibians.

Most of the larger animals of this era were plant-eating mammals. They were preyed upon by carnivores, such as **saber-toothed tigers**. As you are about to discover, these ferocious cats had developed a specialized means of attack.

Savage killers

Saber-toothed tigers must have been among the most savage killers of all time. With their very powerful neck muscles, they would dig their fangs deep into the throat or belly of their unfortunate prey.

Some scientists think **saber-tooths** devoured the entrails and blood of their victims, as well as the flesh.

These fierce creatures may have found it necessary to kill several times each day in order to get enough food to survive.

The victim shown here, fighting for its life against a vicious **saber-toothed tiger**, was an early type of horse that roamed the grasslands of North America. Just imagine what it would have been like to be stabbed by those terrible teeth and claws!

Stuck in

Los Angeles, California, is today one of the busiest cities in the world. Its huge skyscrapers are constantly buzzing with activity. Meanwhile, its suburb of Hollywood is well known as the home of the movie industry.

Who would have thought that in what is now downtown Los Angeles, scientists would make a major discovery about the natural world? In a section of Los Angeles called Rancho La Brea, the bones of about two thousand **saber-toothed tigers** were found.

The dig started in 1913 and lasted twenty years. It yielded the fossilized skeletons of many kinds of birds and other animals — from antelope, mammoths, ground sloths, elephants, and bison to hawks, deer, and wolves. Scientists even discovered the remains of camels, which are no longer found in North America.

Almost eleven thousand years ago, in Pleistocene times, these creatures all became stuck in a large, muddy pit. Oil had been forced up from the lower rock strata in the area, forming a sticky tar from which there was no escape.

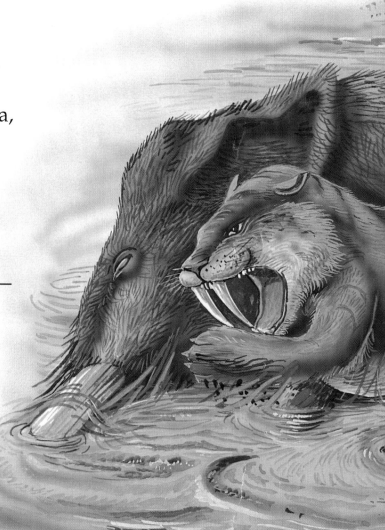

the tar

What probably took place was the herbivores, or plant-eaters, came to what they thought was a lake to drink the water. But they did not stay at the edge of the water. They entered the water and got stuck in the tar. Carnivores then probably came in to prey on the herbivores and also got stuck. This must have happened time and time again, over centuries perhaps, judging from all the skeletons that have been found.

Many of these remains can be seen today in the George C. Page Museum of La Brea Discoveries in Los Angeles, California.

13

The great

During Pleistocene times, many animals migrated from one part of the world to another. Scientists think creatures, such as mammoths, bison, and **saber-toothed tigers**, walked from Europe and Asia to the North American landmass. They walked over what is known as a "land bridge."

Some animals, such as camels, that had evolved in North America, traveled in the other direction. They arrived in Europe and Asia via the same land bridge.

As a result, some animals that now live in one part of the world may have evolved in another.

Toward the end of Pleistocene times, humans also crossed from Asia to the so-called New World (North America) via the same route. Some walked across the ice. If the ice were melting or retreating, the journey may have been made in simple boats.

crossings

Of course, the land bridge was not a *bridge* in the sense that the word is used today. Rather, it was a stretch of land, covered by water at times, that appeared whenever sea levels dropped.

A similar bridge of land had also existed long before Pleistocene times, about seven million years ago. This bridge linked North and South America.

Not all animals made the crossing. Some remained in their forested homes rather than moving on to large, treeless areas.

For instance, the woolly rhinoceros, which lived alongside mammoths in Europe and Asia in Pleistocene times, preferred to stay home.

Apart from **Smilodon**, there were several other prehistoric cats. **Homotherium** (HO-MO-THEER-EE-UM), *below*, roamed Europe, Asia, Africa, and North America in Pleistocene times. Unlike most cats, it walked with its entire foot on the ground, not just the toes. Scientists think it hunted mammoths. Remains of the giant mammoths have been found near those of **Homotherium**.

The **cave lion**, or *Panthera spelaea* (PAN-THERE-AH SPELL-EYE-AH), *below*, lived in Europe in late Pleistocene times. It was bigger than today's lions. It had a long, shaggy coat but shorter teeth than some carnivores. Cave paintings picture the cave lion hunting horses. It probably lived alone and often spent time in caves, where most of its remains have been found.

prehistoric cats

Megantereon (MEG-ANT-ERR-EE-ON), *below*, is more commonly known as the **dirk-toothed** (or **dagger-toothed**) **cat**. This is because of its very long, sharp, canine teeth. It evolved during the Pliocene (PLY-OH-SEEN) era — about five million years ago. **Megantereon** inhabited central and eastern Europe, North America, and southern Africa.

Dinictis felina (DIN-ICT-IS FEL-EEN-AH), *below*, was found in North America during an even earlier age — about thirty million years ago during the Oligocene (OH-LIG-OH-SEEN) era. It had protruding canine teeth that were smaller than **Smilodon**'s, but its thick tail was longer. It was a greatly feared predator.

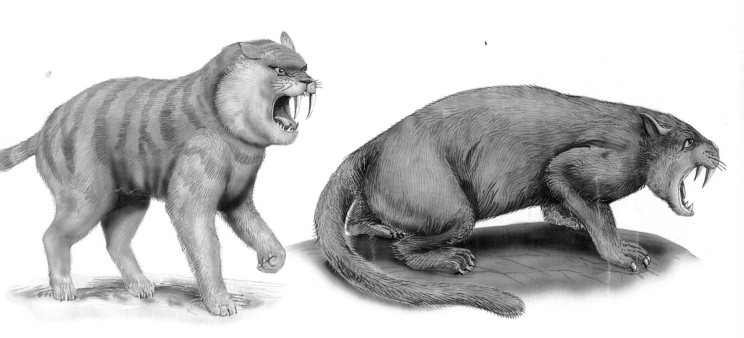

17

Fatal

A group of emperor mammoths — with the scientific name of **Mammuthus imperator** (MAM-OO-THUS IMP-ERR-AH-TOR) — was feeding quietly on the Great Plains of what is now North America.

The tusks of the adult male mammoths were enormous, forming almost complete circles around their heads. If stretched out, these tusks would have been as long as the mammoths were tall.

What incredible creatures they were! The adults stood 13 feet (4 meters) tall — that's more than twice the height of today's average man, and even bigger than the largest African elephants.

It was early morning, and all was fairly still. Herbivores — like this emperor mammoth family – slowly began to nibble on their favorite leaves and plants.

encounter

Then, all at once, the silence of the Pleistocene morning was shattered. As if from nowhere came a mighty roar.

Quick as a flash, four **saber-toothed tigers** leaped at a young mammoth that was a little slower than the rest of its family.

The older mammoths immediately trumpeted a warning. A pack of **saber-toothed tigers** was after the herd.

The baby kicked out with a front foot and threw its head back. It trumpeted as loudly as it could. But it was no use. The young mammoth was soon dead and a meal for the **saber-toothed tigers**.

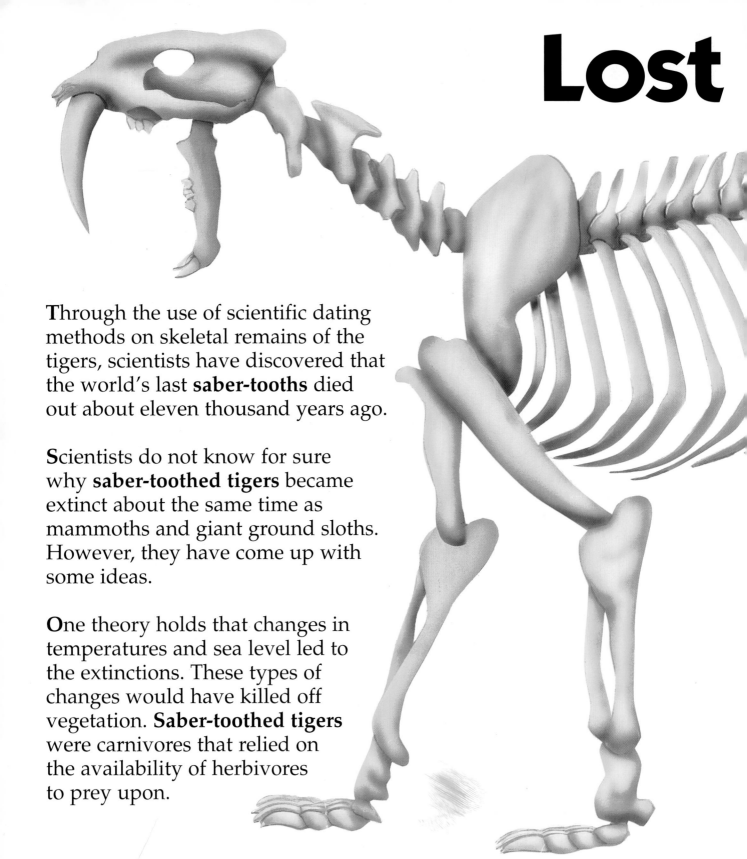

Lost

Through the use of scientific dating methods on skeletal remains of the tigers, scientists have discovered that the world's last **saber-tooths** died out about eleven thousand years ago.

Scientists do not know for sure why **saber-toothed tigers** became extinct about the same time as mammoths and giant ground sloths. However, they have come up with some ideas.

One theory holds that changes in temperatures and sea level led to the extinctions. These types of changes would have killed off vegetation. **Saber-toothed tigers** were carnivores that relied on the availability of herbivores to prey upon.

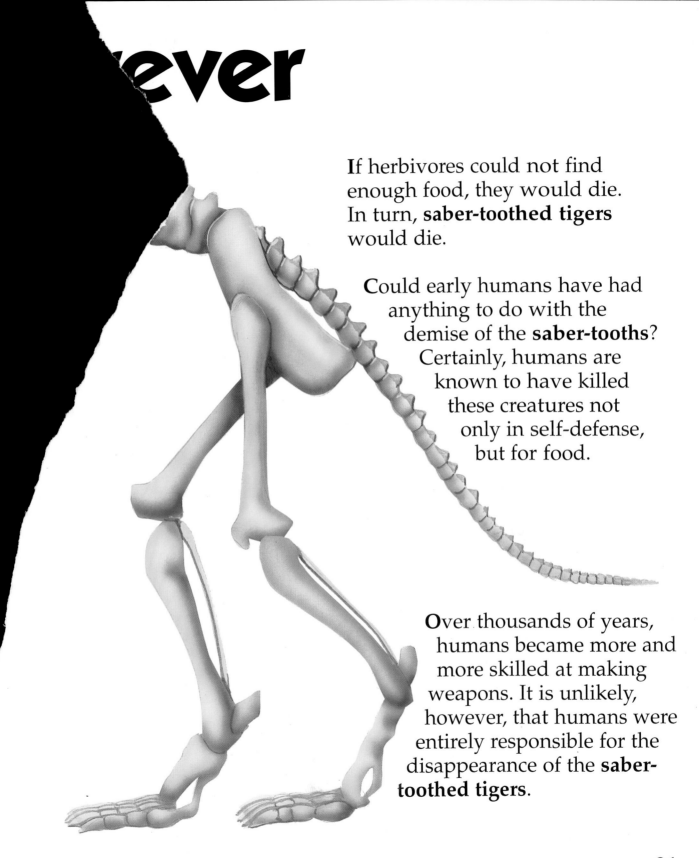

ever

If herbivores could not find enough food, they would die. In turn, **saber-toothed tigers** would die.

Could early humans have had anything to do with the demise of the **saber-tooths**? Certainly, humans are known to have killed these creatures not only in self-defense, but for food.

Over thousands of years, humans became more and more skilled at making weapons. It is unlikely, however, that humans were entirely responsible for the disappearance of the **saber-toothed tigers**.

Saber-tooth

Let's take a look at what scientists know to have been the main features of these prehistoric beasts. They were not giant-sized, but they were vicious.

Strong jaws

Most **saber-toothed tigers** had jaws that opened widely so their teeth could exert a powerful stabbing action. Prey usually bled heavily as a result. Some scientists think the cats drank the blood of their freshly killed victims.

Scimitar teeth

The **saber-tooth** sometimes describ scimitar-like teeth. sword with a large, cu Fossilized remains sho front, upper teeth of **sab tigers** were equally sharp and dangerous. These teeth probably used for biting the and underbelly of a victim.

Powerful legs

Saber-toothed tigers had power legs and could use them forcefull to kick, thereby wounding their victims with sharp claws. Some scientists think these prehistoric cats could run swiftly for short distances only. But scientists also believe that **saber-toothed tigers** preferred to pounce suddenly on their prey, rather than engage in a long chase after a victim.

data

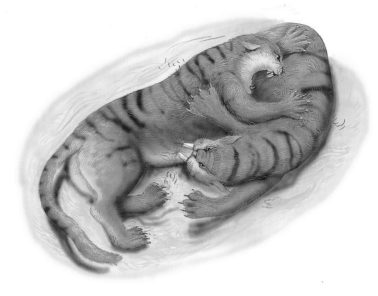

Retractable claws

Some **saber-toothed tigers** — **Smilodon**, for example — had claws that could be held back and out of the way until they were needed for stabbing prey. By moving the upper tendons of the toes, **Smilodon** could make its claws curve up and back, or retract. When it pulled on the lower tendons, the claws would curve down and out. In this position, the claws were ready for stabbing.

Life in packs

Experts believe **saber-toothed tigers** lived and hunted in packs, rather than as individuals. They assume this because so many of the tigers' fossilized skeletons were found close together.

Not always fierce

Some remains show signs of broken teeth and bone injuries, so perhaps **saber-toothed tigers** were not always successful during the hunt. It is also possible that males sometimes fought over the females, as shown *above*.

There are even signs that some elderly **saber-toothed tigers** suffered from arthritis. These individuals probably had difficulty getting around. Living in a pack would have been helpful to them because other tigers might have been willing to share their prey.

Glossary

entrails — an animal's digestive organs.

fangs — the long, front canine teeth of a carnivore, or meat-eating animal.

Mammuthus imperator — a huge, elephant-like creature with giant tusks that lived in North America long ago.

Oligocene age — a period of time before the Pliocene and Pleistocene ages, over 30 million years ago.

Pleistocene age — a period of time that lasted from about 2 million years ago to about 10,000 B.C. This time period included the great Ice Age.

Pliocene age — a period of time that began before the Pleistocene age, about 5 million years ago.

Rancho La Brea — a region of Los Angeles, California, where the remains of two thousand saber-toothed tigers have been found. Remains of many other prehistoric animals were found there, as well.

Smilodon — the most common type of saber-toothed tiger.

tendon — a band of tissue by which muscle is attached to bone.

Index